Praise for
At Water's Edge: Poems of Lake Nebagamon

In these engaging poems, Louis Daniel Brodsky continues the meditative dialogue with Lake Nebagamon and its environs, which he began in *You Can't Go Back, Exactly*. Reading *At Water's Edge*, one thinks of Thoreau in his cabin near Walden Pond, or Wordsworth in London, reflecting on his boyhood haunts in the Lake District, or Whitman on his Long Island beach. But the backdrop of Brodsky's Nebagamon poems, as one knows from his previous books, is thoroughly modern; and the driven need, at times desperate, to escape the loneliness, alienation, and dizziness of the urban "necropolis" both underscores and heightens the personal quest for inner peace and serenity that the poet finds in the north Wisconsin woods.

— Robert Hamblin, author of *Keeping Score: Sports Poems for Every Season*; *This House, This Town: One Couple's Love Affair with an Old House and a Historic Town*; and *Crossroads: Poems of a Mississippi Childhood*

At Water's Edge opens, for us, a full sense of love for the outdoors, from someone generously "Taking time to look and listen, see and hear." Poem after poem shares one man's alerted words for the American north country and for our journeying moods of mind and body, in this ever-changing natural world.

— John Felstiner, author of *Can Poetry Save the Earth?: A Field Guide to Nature Poems*; *Paul Celan: Poet, Survivor, Jew*; and *Translating Neruda: The Way to Macchu Picchu*

Perhaps the only thing as dear to Louis Daniel Brodsky as the beauty of the written word are his memories and experiences on the shores of Wisconsin's Lake Nebagamon, which the poet describes as "glory's hinterlands." The combination of his two passions is a wonderful example of the poetry of place — the kind of soul-forming and life-affirming locale that we all have somewhere in our lives. What the open road was to Whitman, the North Woods are to Brodsky.

— Brad Herzog, author of *Turn Left at the Trojan Horse*

I have been a longtime admirer of the poems of Louis Daniel Brodsky, but no collection of his has quite moved me as deeply as *At Water's Edge*. These poems bring us, his grateful readers, closer to the experience of nature, which is, as Emerson noted, a symbol of spirit. Spirit and nature mingle in these poems, which lift us, lay us bare. I hope Brodsky finds a wide audience for this work.

— Jay Parini, author of *The Art of Subtraction: New and Selected Poems* and *Promised Land: Thirteen Books That Changed America*

You give such great local color to our wonderful little village, camp, trees, birds, lake, etc. I really feel the longing and the depth of your emotions in each selection. . . . Lake Nebagamon is fortunate to have you write about our little town.

— Eddie Drolson, lifelong resident of Lake Nebagamon, Wisconsin

As one may describe Bouguereau to the blind or Ravel to the deaf, Brodsky relates the amniotic splendor of Lake Nebagamon and the freedom found in the captivity of its ecstatic peace. I know Brodsky's lake as if I've swum her since birth, yet I long for the day when I can know my Nebagamon and can compare it to this poet's envy-worthy testimony. I must trust his promise of discovery: "When you look for it – / That which you'll never find – / It'll be there, waiting for you."

— David Herrle, editor of *SubtleTea.com* and author of *Abyssinia, Jill Rush*

Louis Daniel Brodsky is our Whitman of the Middle West. His poetry rings out from the heart of the heartland, full of tenderness, truth, and a wholly American beauty, reminding us that grace is a possibility, even for our sore-beset land and its troubled people.

—James Howard Kunstler, author of *The Long Emergency* and *World Made by Hand*

At Water's Edge

Books by Louis Daniel Brodsky

Poetry

Five Facets of Myself   (1967)* (1995)

The Easy Philosopher   (1967)* (1995)

"A Hard Coming of It" and Other Poems   (1967)* (1995)

The Foul Rag-and-Bone Shop   (1967)* (1969, exp.)* (1995, exp.)

Points in Time   (1971)* (1995) (1996)

Taking the Back Road Home   (1972)* (1997) (2000)

Trip to Tipton and Other Compulsions   (1973)* (1997)

"The Talking Machine" and Other Poems   (1974)* (1997)

Tiffany Shade   (1974)* (1997)

Trilogy: A Birth Cycle   (1974) (1998)

Cold Companionable Streams   (1975)* (1999)

Monday's Child   (1975) (1998)

Preparing for Incarnations   (1975)* (1976, exp.) (1999) (1999, exp.)

The Kingdom of Gewgaw   (1976) (2000)

Point of Americas II   (1976) (1998)

La Preciosa   (1977) (2001)

Stranded in the Land of Transients   (1978) (2000)

The Uncelebrated Ceremony of Pants-Factory Fatso   (1978) (2001)

Birds in Passage   (1980) (2001)

Résumé of a Scrapegoat   (1980) (2001)

Mississippi Vistas: Volume One of *A Mississippi Trilogy*   (1983) (1990)

You Can't Go Back, Exactly   (1988, two eds.) (1989) (2003, exp.)

The Thorough Earth   (1989)

Four and Twenty Blackbirds Soaring   (1989)

Falling from Heaven: Holocaust Poems of a Jew and a Gentile *(with William Heyen)*   (1991)

Forever, for Now: Poems for a Later Love   (1991)

Mistress Mississippi: Volume Three of *A Mississippi Trilogy*   (1992)

A Gleam in the Eye: Volume One of *The Seasons of Youth*   (1992) (2009)

Gestapo Crows: Holocaust Poems   (1992)

The Capital Café: Poems of Redneck, U.S.A.   (1993)

Disappearing in Mississippi Latitudes: Volume Two of *A Mississippi Trilogy*   (1994)

A Mississippi Trilogy: A Poetic Saga of the South   (1995)*

Paper-Whites for Lady Jane: Poems of a Midlife Love Affair   (1995)

The Complete Poems of Louis Daniel Brodsky: Volume One, 1963–1967
   (edited by Sheri L. Vandermolen)   (1996)

Three Early Books of Poems by Louis Daniel Brodsky, 1967–1969: *The Easy Philosopher,*
   "A Hard Coming of It" and Other Poems, and *The Foul Rag-and-Bone Shop*
   (edited by Sheri L. Vandermolen)   (1997)

The Eleventh Lost Tribe: Poems of the Holocaust   (1998)

Toward the Torah, Soaring: Poems of the Renascence of Faith   (1998)

Voice Within the Void: Poems of *Homo supinus*   (2000)

Rabbi Auschwitz: Poems of the Shoah   (2000)* (2009)

The Swastika Clock: Endlösung Poems   (2001)*

Shadow War: A Poetic Chronicle of September 11 and Beyond, Volume One   (2001) (2004)

The Complete Poems of Louis Daniel Brodsky: Volume Two, 1967–1976
   (edited by Sheri L. Vandermolen)   (2002)

Shadow War: A Poetic Chronicle of September 11 and Beyond, Volume Two   (2002) (2004)

Shadow War: A Poetic Chronicle of September 11 and Beyond, Volume Three   (2002) (2004)

Shadow War: A Poetic Chronicle of September 11 and Beyond, Volume Four   (2002) (2004)

Shadow War: A Poetic Chronicle of September 11 and Beyond, Volume Five   (2002) (2004)

Heavenward   (2003)*

Regime Change: Poems of America's Showdown with Iraq, Volume One   (2003)*

Regime Change: Poems of America's Showdown with Iraq, Volume Two   (2003)*

Regime Change: Poems of America's Showdown with Iraq, Volume Three   (2003)*

The Complete Poems of Louis Daniel Brodsky: Volume Three, 1976–1980
   (edited by Sheri L. Vandermolen)   (2004)

Peddler on the Road: Days in the Life of Willy Sypher   (2005)

Combing Florida's Shores: Poems of Two Lifetimes   (2006)

Showdown with a Cactus: Poems Chronicling the Prickly Struggle Between the Forces
   of Dubya-ness and Enlightenment, 2003–2006   (2006)

A Transcendental Almanac: Poems of Nature   (2006)

Once upon a Small-Town Time: Poems of America's Heartland   (2007)

Still Wandering in the Wilderness: Poems of the Jewish Diaspora   (2007)

The Location of the Unknown: Shoah Poems   (2008)*

The World Waiting to Be: Poems About the Creative Process   (2008)

The Complete Poems of Louis Daniel Brodsky: Volume Four, 1981–1985
   (edited by Sheri L. Vandermolen)   (2008)

Dine-Rite: Breakfast Poems   (2008)

Kampf: Poems of the Holocaust   (2009)*

By Leaps and Bounds: Volume Two of *The Seasons of Youth*   (2009)

At Water's Edge: Poems of Lake Nebagamon, Volume One   (2010)

Bibliography (coedited with Robert Hamblin)

Selections from the William Faulkner Collection of Louis Daniel Brodsky: A Descriptive
   Catalogue   (1979)

Faulkner: A Comprehensive Guide to the Brodsky Collection: Volume I, The Biobibliography   (1982)

Faulkner: A Comprehensive Guide to the Brodsky Collection: Volume II, The Letters   (1984)

Faulkner: A Comprehensive Guide to the Brodsky Collection: Volume III, *The De Gaulle Story*   (1984)

Faulkner: A Comprehensive Guide to the Brodsky Collection: Volume IV, *Battle Cry*   (1985)

Bibliography *(coedited with Robert Hamblin)*

Faulkner: A Comprehensive Guide to the Brodsky Collection: Volume V, Manuscripts and
   Documents   (1989)

Stallion Road: A Screenplay by William Faulkner   (1989)

Country Lawyer and Other Stories for the Screen by William Faulkner   (1987)

Biography

William Faulkner, Life Glimpses   (1990)

Fiction

Between Grief and Nothing *(novel)*   (1964)*

Between the Heron and the Wren *(novel)*   (1965)*

"Dink Phlager's Alligator" and Other Stories   (1966)*

The Drift of Things *(novel)*   (1966)*

Vineyard's Toys *(novel)*   (1967)*

The Bindle Stiffs *(novel)*   (1968)*

Yellow Bricks *(short fictions)*   (1999)

Catchin' the Drift o' the Draft *(short fictions)*   (1999)

This Here's a Merica *(short fictions)*   (1999)

Leaky Tubs *(short fictions)*   (2001)

Rated Xmas *(short fictions)*   (2003)

Nuts to You! *(short fictions)*   (2004)

Pigskinizations *(short fictions)*   (2005)

With One Foot in the Butterfly Farm *(short fictions)*   (2009)

Memoir

The Adventures of the Night Riders, Better Known as the Terrible Trio
   (with Richard Milsten)   (1961)*

* *Unpublished*

At Water's Edge

Poems of Lake Nebagamon,
Volume One

Louis Daniel Brodsky

Time Being BookS

An imprint of Time Being Press
St. Louis, Missouri

Time Being Books®
10411 Clayton Road
St. Louis, Missouri 63131

Time Being Books® is an imprint of Time Being Press®, St. Louis, Missouri.

Time Being Press® is a 501(c)(3) not-for-profit corporation.

Time Being Books® volumes are printed on acid-free paper.

ISBN 978-1-56809-126-6 (paperback)

Library of Congress Cataloging-in-Publication Data:

Brodsky, Louis Daniel.
    At water's edge : poems of Lake Nebagamon / by Louis Daniel Brodsky. — 1st ed.
        v. cm.
        ISBN: 978-1-56809-126-6 (v. 1 : pbk. : alk. paper) 1. Nature--Poetry. 2. Lake Nebagamon (Wis. : Village)--Poetry. 3. Wisconsin--Poetry. I. Title. II. Title: Poems of Lake Nebagamon. III. Title: Lake Nebagamon.
    PS3552.R623A93 2010
    811'.54—dc22
                                                        2010011682

Cover design by Jeff Hirsch
Cover photo copyrighted by and reprinted with permission of
    Troika Brodsky
Book design and typesetting by Trilogy M. Mattson

Manufactured in the United States of America
First Edition, first printing (2010)

Acknowledgments

I am so very grateful to Sheri Vandermolen and Jerry Call, my long-time editors at Time Being Books, who enlightened me, in so many ways, as this book evolved over three years. Without their insights and overviews augmenting mine, my passion for the land I evoke never would have been adequately translated, shaped to the page.

My thanks to Michael Brodsky, for his close reading of, and suggestions for, the first two sections of this book, and for introducing me to the beautifully lyrical works of Sigurd F. Olson.

I'm grateful to the following publications, in which these poems appeared, in earlier versions: *Avocet* ("The Lake," "The Lord of the Forest," and "Poet in a Cabin"); *The Cape Rock* ("The Loons of Lake Nebagamon"); *First Time* ("Ripples and Gusts"); *New Laurel Review* ("Poet in a Cabin"); *Poem* ("The Leaves"); *Poetry NZ* ("The Stranger"); and *Stray Branch* ("The Passing Past").

For my beloved son, Troika.

May you and I

"Keep the fires burning!"

Contents

Each of us has an Up North. It's a time and place far from the here and now. It's a map on the wall, a dream in the making, a tugging at one's soul. For those who feel the tug, who make the dream happen, who put the map in the packsack and go, the world is never quite the same again.
— Sam Cook, *Up North*

Over all was the silence of the wilderness, that sense of oneness which comes only when there are no distracting sights or sounds, when we listen with inward ears and see with inward eyes, when we feel and are aware with our entire beings rather than our senses.
— Sigurd F. Olson, *The Singing Wilderness*

The Village, the Lake, and the Woods

The Cabin

Autumn Comes to Lake Nebagamon

At Water's Edge

Late September

I. Bless Me and Me Alone

Bless me and me alone,
This benign morning, in northern Wisconsin.
I've fulfilled myself,
With a prophecy of golden timelessness,
Albeit a vision but five days long:

A getaway to a cabin on a remote lake,
Where silence is the epiphany of this protean season,
When life listens to the autumnal summoning
And the sun casts its net over the shore-lapping waters,
Certain to catch my amazement swimming in its gaze.

Just being away, cut loose from routine, secluded,
Liberated from the hurly-burly of world events
(To which I bow daily, in pagan worship,
As if addicted to the Lorelei fix that politicians promise —
Harmonizing Earth's cacophony),

Revitalizes my harried spirit,
Allows me to slow my helter-skelter breath,
Examine, if not who I've been, these past few decades,
What identity my heart might assume
In the intimate future left to my creative shaping.

Bless me and me alone,
For recognizing the necessity to step outside of time,
Though briefly, realizing that I, not it,
Can't afford to rush to conclusions,
Especially if I intend to devote myself to perpetuity.

II. Chalice

Yesterday morning,
Lake Nebagamon was a fiery chalice,
Its ripples aflame with the sun's mirrored corona.

Less than twenty-four hours later,
A somber steady drizzle
Trickles through day's diaphanous hourglass,

Its grains of sand-rain
Thumping gently on the roof of my shore-hugging cabin,
Beading up on imagination's windows.

The scurrying sky seems to be in a determined hurry
(Chasing or chased, impossible to infer),
Exposing infinite layers of its spirit.

I'm glad all I have to do, today, is stay put
And revel in Wisconsin's rapture,
As it blesses my naked soul with its sweetest balms.

III. The Stranger

This composed, isolated lake,
Where I've eavesdropped on nature,
These past three days and nights,
Has an infinite number of lives,
If not many, many more. I know! I know!

For instance, just an hour ago,
When I awoke from slumber's deep release,
I discovered the water's still surface filling my gaze,
The vivid dappling of the far shore's trees
Impastoed halfway across its glassy canvas.

Now, having finished breakfast, I return to my perch,
In this many-windowed cabin.
The mist-enshrouded lake
Has metamorphosed into a venerable old fish,
Leaping, flailing, lashing, as if caught on a line.

Only the trees across from me, lackluster, blurred,
Are faintly visible, for the roiling.
If I wait (I have no place to go, to be),
The lake might reshape itself
Into the stranger who looks and acts just like me.

IV. Just Down the Road

Just down the rough-tarred road,
About a quarter-mile from where I'm staying,
In this rented cabin on the shore of Lake Nebagamon,
Slumbers the boys' summer camp,
Desolate, lonely, lamenting its necessary quiescence.

On a lark or just with curiosity's spark,
I wend my way toward its back gate,
Wander in, not as a trespasser,
Anymore than wind, chipmunks, skunks, and snow
Could be considered interlopers in this refuge,

Rather as a pilgrim come, in humbleness, reverence,
Not to disturb the slightest pine needle or stone
But to peek into a world utterly remote from mine,
Attempt to envision the lives that have resided here,
Amidst these vertiginous pine trees.

Empty white cabins on cement-block foundations,
With moss-strewn shingles, holey screens, invite me in.
I open five or six green doors.
Their single springs groan,
Speak to me, in a plaintive language from long ago.

I peer into these dark reliquaries,
The bunk beds shouldering dilapidated mattresses,
The rafters devoid of duffel bags,
The walls covered with plaques decades dusty —
Names of those who've graced the premises.

In every direction, root-clotted paths meander.
My eyes try to decide which to take.
Its all a colossal maze, a wild steeplechase
Leading from tennis courts to council ring and range,
Rec hall to the Big House, on the hill,

And down again, to the lake, the back gate,
The rough-tarred road
Connecting the boys' purlieus with my cabin,
About a quarter-mile up East Waterfront Drive,
Where I've been staying, for days,

Hoping that before memory grows too old to care,
I might catch even a dim glimpse
Of the child within the man I am,
Who began his first of fourteen camp summers
Just down the road, fifty-five years from here.

V. Baptism by Pine Needles

It's not much above fifty, this Sunday morning,
As I amble through the camp.
Seeing my breath could be the closest I come to worship.

Sun funneling, asymmetrically, through the pines,
Dapples the turf, with shadows and light,
Accentuates the strangest rain:

A shower of brown needles,
Brushing my neck, hands, landing in my hair,
Anointing me with the trees' divinity.

VI. After the Rain

Again, the sun,
After two days of drizzle mixed with downpour.
I step outdoors, into dawn's exquisite crispness.

Though it's been six hours since the rain dissipated,
Its beads still drip off pine needles, eaves,
Everything between blue sky and brown-green ground.

The lake is a stage with shimmering scrim curtains —
Steam rising as sheets of mist,
Disappearing into morning's sonorous calm.

And in this land, so far away from who I am,
I'm at peace with all that's left for me to get done
Before the sun sets my stone in place.

Lake Nebagamon Sojourn

I. Ripples and Gusts

I always thought the wind was invisible
And, if not audible, at least articulate.
The trees know this best; they whisper its lyrics.

But sitting at dock's end,
I see the breeze as basket-weave ripples
On the surface of this restless lake,

Watch its gusts skitter across the water,
Forming, thrusting, shifting,
Then winnowing into diminishment, welling again.

Out here, I sense my hour is now,
Though I'm not even wearing a wrist watch;
Indeed, I've forgotten to zip my fly.

At sixty-six
(Almost as old as the temperature is brisk),
I'm just a mess, a fool of a poet,

Who, perhaps for the first time in his life,
Has seen the wind face to face —
Lake Nebagamon's ripples and gusts.

II. Redolence

Sitting on this unforgivingly rigid white Adirondack chair,
Just one of a dozen
On which the more meditative boys occasionally light,

To let the day dream itself serenely away,
I breathe in the deep opiate scent of pine trees
Inundating Camp Nebagamon's sanctuary,

That unmistakable fragrance I've known since my tenth year,
When I began my two-month disappearances from St. Louis,
Into upper Wisconsin's pristine simplicity.

Over the decades, I've returned to visit these grounds
And always willed my imagination to capture enough of this aroma
To take home with me, in time's vial,

So that whenever aging threatens to upstage my psyche,
Bring me to my shaky knees, at its altar,
I need simply to release its redolence, and I'm revitalized.

This out-of-time July afternoon,
My sense of smell is overwhelmed.
Apparently, long ago, these North Woods scent-marked my soul.

Today, I can't help noticing
That the trees are keenly aware of my presence, far below.
I'm a natural part of their territory.

III. Lake Nebagamon Dusk

From where I peer, this Saturday twilight,
On the deck of the town's best restaurant,
I can view the entire municipal swimming hole.

Just below the red-split-log auditorium,
Where all of the community's civic activities occur,
The lawn, sloping down to the shore,

Is dizzy with swimsuited kids
Darting in and out of their loud shouts and screams,
Like dragonflies and water striders,

While their parents conspire above the fray,
Digesting gossip, comparing unharried agendas.
I delight in my role as outsider; it keeps me free,

Allows me to invent, enter, others' lives,
Render them, with empathy,
Without having to spend too much time and energy.

Not yet forty-eight hours in my cabin, at water's edge,
I already feel like an acknowledged native,
A village member in good standing.

By tomorrow of my six-day stay,
Most likely I'll have decided not to return home,
Rather to settle in, for an extended absence.

Meanwhile, this night, which has begun young,
Has an endless trajectory to go, before I seek sleep,
To reassure myself this dream isn't a dream.

IV. I'm Here

Sunday morning in Lake Nebagamon
Isn't appreciably different from one anywhere else.
People are sleeping in; birds are at matins.

Solemnity pervades this day of rest.
Church bells gently punctuate the air,
Reassuring the villagers that God's spirit is near.

The water and trees lullaby each other,
With immemorial adoration.
The sky's blue hue shelters Earth from the universe.

I see my shadow shadowing me, in the shallows.
I'd recognize it anywhere;
We've been inseparable, six and a half decades.

Every once in a once-in-a-while,
A motorboat, far against the opposite shore,
Unleashes waves that reach this dock,

Rock it ever so slightly,
Reminding me I'm here, in northern Wisconsin,
Where time invites me to lose myself.

V. Serene Evening

Though this lake says nothing,
It dominates these North Woods surrounds,
Like a great oracular voice,

As if everything, for shorelined miles around,
Were drawn into its force,
Toward its mystical core, its origins.

It casts a reverberant spell
Over all of us who dwell in the aura of its swell.
We pay obeisance to its fluid sovereignty,

By reconciling our rhythms with its subtle surge,
Consigning our lives into its keeping,
Trusting that its dominion will protect us,

Let no primal curses compromise our spirits
Or cause us to forsake our allegiance
By seeking to leave this never unseasonable purlieu.

Amidst this twilight's blessed circumambience,
I give thanks to the quietude,
For letting me devote my soul to these waters,

Spend my span translating their undulations,
Learning their ineffable ways,
So that one night, just like this serene evening,

I might simply disappear,
Commit my spirit to the placid fathoms of this lake,
As the sun retrieves its reflections and sleeps.

VI. Perfect Weather

In my inexpert estimation,
If ever there were perfect weather,
It would have to be found here, this July,

In the village of Lake Nebagamon,
Where the breeze keeps the waters stirred,
Rustles the trees, with a soothing seventy degrees.

Then again, maybe I'm just being frivolous,
Effusing over something the folks in this clime
Assume to be their entitlement.

But the lower Midwest, which I left, four days ago,
Swelters in unbreathable humidity
(Long ago, we St. Louisans ceased calling it "heat").

This sundown, relaxing on Lawn Beach Inn's deck,
Overlooking the lake at rest,
I predict perfect weather for tonight's forever.

VII. Feeding Time

Wisps of clouds linger in the night sky,
Some scattered strands tinged pink,
Several blotches gray, on the still-blue blotter.

Imagine; it's ten minutes after nine,
And despite this welkin's enduring brightness,
I can see Venus, pulsing on the horizon.

A lone canoeist paddles past, in the distance,
As I sit on the bench at the end of my dock,
Captivated by the docility of this lake.

His J-strokes set ripples astir;
They crawl across the water, reach me.
I'm astonished.

In my mind's 360-degree panorama,
I make eye contact
With lights radiating from every shoreline cabin,

And I feel as if we're all kindred spirits,
Those of us who share this lake,
Partake of its hushed, majestic essence.

Suddenly, a fish kisses the surface; then others.
Now, stars are penetrating the darkness.
It's my soul's feeding time, too.

VIII. Storm's Progress

Across the lake, above Honeymoon Point,
Voluminous cumulus clouds —
Empyreal Himalayan peaks

Mottled gray-blue against white —
Are slanting black rain in this direction.
A brisk wind is at its back,

Cooling things, stirring up a chop,
Warning all of us in this village
That a downpour is about to riot.

Tonight, the stars will stay hidden.
Sleep should have no difficulty finding me,
Despite drops staccatoing my roof.

Just now, however, hunkered down, on the dock,
I've got to finish this poem.
If not, the storm will never progress.

IX. The Lake Awakens

Though it seems late — 7:30 a.m. —
The lake is decidedly not yet awake.
There's nothing etching its surface.

It might as well be the sky,
For all the perfectly mirrored clouds
Marbling its absolute smoothness.

The only sounds, for eternities around,
Are birds singing ancestral chants,
As if to let me know I'm invited.

Just now, a lone gull,
Having strayed from Lake Superior, flies by.
Fish, at feeding, release concentric circles.

In the distance, a bell rends the silence —
It's the boys' camp, down the road,
Calling its charges to embrace the day —

Followed by voices yelling, in unison,
"Evvv-ry bod-y riiiise and shiiiine!
Rollll out, rollll out!"

Suddenly, heat stings my back.
When I look at the lake again, it's cloudless.
Two ducks glide by.

A young couple, three houses down,
Navigates the wooden dock;
Their dog splashes a path through the water.

A second bell riffles the serenity.
It must be calling the kids to breakfast.
Now, it's time for me to decide what comes next.

X. Disoriented

Home,
I confess to still being disoriented.
I'm not sure if this is St. Louis or Lake Nebagamon,

Where, just days ago, I simplified my soul,
In a cabin hugging the shore,
Did whatever I pleased — slept till whenever,

Gave no heed to schedules, agendas, protocols,
Let my precious energy spend itself
Investing in daydreams, lollygagging the hours away,

Not once speculating on the future,
Brooding on the past, estimating the present,
Rather measuring time as clouds crossing the sky.

This evening in late July,
Sequestered in a booth, within this noisy café,
I wonder whether my spirit is in Missouri

Or thirty miles southeast of Duluth,
Where I'm forgetting who I am, have been,
Assuming ownership of seventy feet of shoreline

That defines my estate,
In Wisconsin's demesne of white birches and pines.
My senses can't disentangle *then* from *now*.

Maybe the answer will materialize at sunrise,
When I peer out my bedroom windows
And register either rush-hour traffic or passive lake water.

In that raucous or peaceful moment,
I'll know into whose embrace I've been delivered,
Whether my destiny is arrested or yet has time to grow.

The Woods

I. The Waves

All afternoon and deep into gloaming's shadows,
Lake Nebagamon's waves kept surging shoreward,
Like legions of Roman soldiers

Engaged in a battle to the death.
That they'd mistaken me for their enemy
Seemed highly implausible,

Since similes have no mind of their own,
Can't comprehend the subtleties of figurative language,
Which make possible such transformations.

And yet, that's how they perceived me,
Because they continuously broke into my meditations,
Like common thieves, and stole my concentration,

Until, finally, in a peak of inutterable frustration,
I slammed closed my notebook, gathered up my gear,
And went indoors, to wait for the waves to dissipate.

They never really did,
Rather kept inundating my sleep, my dreams,
As rain pelting the roof and windows of my cabin.

II. Water Spirits

Morning's cold, gray clouds
Cast such wayward shades over the lake,
I thought this day had forsaken me.

But by noon, the blue welkin,
Hidden above the swift-scudding fluff,
Broke through myriad openings,

And rays flecked the ruffled surface,
With sparks refracting off the waves,
Like fire flashing from a diamond's facets,

Glitter skittering from skyrockets,
Or magical dust scattering from a fairy's wand —
"Water spirits," Chippewas once called them.

With their tribal dances,
Those thousands of miniature suns dazzled me,
Long after the hours ascended to starry night.

III. Secrets

Warmth that embraced me, three months ago,
On my last visit to this clime, is gone.
And though September's chill has arrived,

I find myself back in this tiny community,
Lured here, by its resident trinity:
Tranquillity, solitude, and timelessness.

I've invested much of this brisk afternoon
Letting curiosity and reminiscence
Hike through the shuttered boys' camp,

Guide my acolyte's spirit into densities
Teeming with secrets of pines, spruces, cedars,
Ashes and white birches fallen into pungent decay,

Decomposing bark, wood, needles, and leaves
Taking the shapes of soft paths
Meandering through this abandoned land,

Leading me back to where my manhood began,
Home, to this lake, these cabins, these coverts,
Where nature taught me her rituals and myths,

How to handle stress, pain, failure, success,
Maintain equanimity and faith,
Meditate on rose-window sunsets.

This glorious afternoon has guided me to twilight,
Twilight to the ecstasy of trees, water, sky,
The epiphany of shapes, colors, sounds, smells,

These elements of life to night, night to afterlife,
Afterlife to the reality of rain clouds
Floating in, hovering above Lake Nebagamon.

IV. A Walk in the Woods

After last night's rain,
The fallen trees give off a sweet musk;
Spider webs, grass, and ferns glisten;

Mushrooms have sprouted;
Sphagnum paths are spongy underfoot;
Only the lake, still low, seems untouched.

It doesn't take a naturalist
To sense change in the crisp air —
Reddening maple leaves prophesy it.

Exiting the density of this pristine purlieu,
I pause to admire two giant cedars side by side
(Husband and wife of maybe eighty years)

And a sparse stand of Norway spruces,
Whose arched bows, their needles drooping,
Attest to a century of blessed perpetuation.

Soon, I return to my starting point,
At the edge of civilization —
The front entrance to the empty boys' camp —

And try to recalibrate myself with time,
Realign who I am
With whom, two hours ago, I left behind,

And hope to find, in the great white egret
Flying by, low along the shoreline,
Or in the quacking mallards zigzagging past my dock

Or in the squadron of turkey buzzards
Wheeling so close to the cloud cover,
I can almost see their feathers rubbing off fluff . . .

Hope to divine, in these birds,
A sign that the land's imminent hibernation
Will protect all its creatures, including me.

V. Animal Instincts

In these upper reaches,
I could easily be a chipmunk scampering over pine needles,
A squirrel on a tree trunk, evading my shadow,

Or a possum, an otter, a deer, a raccoon, a skunk,
Possibly a red fox, a black bear, but not a snake,
Though I could be a worm or a slug.

I suppose that something primal awakens in me,
When I'm so far away from the city,
Where, mostly, I reside in isolation from nature.

Perhaps it's that here, civilization isn't so blatant,
That a shred of the vestigial animal in me
Emerges from my deepest dreams, reinhabits my atoms,

Calls me back, to my beginnings,
To taste the primitive virtues of instinctive coexistence
With creatures who spend all their active hours

Foraging for sustenance, keeping cool or warm,
Surviving the ever-prevalent threat of predators,
Propagating their species, and sheltering their young,

Until the day comes when their rhythms quit them
And they disappear into the consummate decay,
Which reclaims them, for the primordial woods.

Oh, how I long for a circling turkey buzzard
Or commanding bald eagle
To swoop down and clutch my spirit, in its talons,

Carry it off to some coniferous pinnacle,
Where, all day and night,
I'd know how it feels to nurture life, being devoured.

VI. The Doe

Settled, now, I reflect on my midday hike —
The young and stunning white-tailed doe
That let me come within twenty feet,

Before it retreated into the sun-splattered underbrush,
Not in a rush but with hushed nonchalance,
As though I were just another tree in its midst.

Surely there must have been more than the one deer
Lurking in those still-green-leafy recesses;
Only, none appeared during the rest of my traipse,

Although every footstep of the way,
I kept anticipating seeing it, its mate, its herd,
Wondering if what I'd encountered was innocence —

A natural symbol of this land's divinity,
Sunday's sublimity, my heart's apotheosis —
Or just a doe, here and gone, in a pivot and a leap.

VII. Reading the Water Spirits

Sitting outdoors, this matchless autumn afternoon,
Reading, like tea leaves, the water spirits
Glinting off the tips of the lake's rippling surface,

My flannel shirt absorbing the protean sun,
Whose crisp sixty-five degrees
Render this Wisconsin interlude visceral, tangible,

I'm compelled to believe, finally,
That despite an interminable spell of office claustrophobia,
There *is* hope for my insentient soul,

Which bartered its precious emotions,
For the safe, numbing satiety of society's comforts.
From today, all my heart's tomorrows will dawn here.

VIII. Writing on the Wall

Camp Nebagamon for Boys
Stands at the entrance to the woods I roam,
In hope of unlocking a few more sylvan mysteries,

Interviewing some of the denizens —
Mushrooms, chipmunks, lichens and mosses,
Perhaps a black bear, a white-tailed deer.

I'm sure the sumacs, cedars, pines, tamaracks, and ashes
Will acquiesce to my intimate inquiries.
Doubtless, the lake will yield to my investigations.

But this afternoon, I don't get that deep into the recesses —
Not at first, anyway — for lingering at the peripheries,
Revisiting the ten cabins in which I spent summer months,

Over fourteen seasons running,
When the boy in me attended to the requisites of manhood,
Wrote, on the walls of each of these habitations,

His "Kilroy Was Here,"
As if to leave a record, testify, to the future,
So that my legacy, somehow, would live in perpetuity,

For having been monumental, quintessential,
Indispensable to the orderly scheme of life itself,
The spark at the heart of the harmonious universe.

But to my hyperbolized chagrin
(After all, that bravado played out fifty years ago),
When I search for my signatures and dates,

I find that the names from my era have been painted over,
The walls now shouting forth, in vibrant colors,
Newer appellations of hubristic youth,

Effectively canceling my existence in camp's history
And making me wonder if I was ever here.
Only after slamming the screen door of the last cabin

Do I head off for the timeless woods,
Hoping that, there, at least,
I'll discover something that remembers me from the past.

IX. One More Dream

I awaken, with Lake Nebagamon
Flowing through my windows, into my bedroom,
Gently nudging the beached driftwood of my dreams,

As if it has intentions of eventually transporting,
Back to its core,
A large part of my heart, on its invisible, ceaseless ebb.

After all, in these oneiric vestiges
Lies a six-day accumulation of mystical essences,
Which I gathered from my hikes in the nearby woods,

Where I mined nature's revelations, to my mind's delight,
Mesmerized by the conversations growth and decay exchanged,
The dialogues between resident animals and flora —

Weaving spiders; birds flitting between deep-green obscurities;
Lime- and brown-hued mosses clinging to the ground;
Downed trunks rotting into fist-sized chunks;

Scurrying chipmunks; black squirrels barking angrily at me;
Poplar and birch leaves murmuring to the breezes;
Sinister-looking fungal shapes peering out, everywhere;

Pileated woodpeckers stitching the thick undergrowth,
In threads of red, black, and white;
Deer; otters; foxes; skunks; raccoons; possums.

But now, what I realize most palpably,
As the waves tug at my reluctant spirit, summon me to arise,
Is that I'm about to leave behind these enchanted woods,

Return to my citified life, for a protracted passage of longing.
And all I can do to forestall it
Is fall back asleep, for one more dream.

X. Last Friday's Twilight

One long-ago week ago tonight,
Almost seven hundred miles north
Of this cacophonous *here and now*,

I sat on Lawn Beach Inn's deck,
As twilight descended over the village,
And witnessed sunset pastel Lake Nebagamon,

In oranges, pinks, indigos, and violets —
Sensations of sublimity and plenitude
That blended with the wine I was sipping,

Rendering my soul whole, transcendent.
For a suspended eon,
I relaxed there, lost hold of my identity.

So invested was I,
In that communion with the lake's spirit,
Its blood filling my grateful veins,

That I deluded myself into believing
I'd never return to from wherever I'd come,
Not twenty-four hours earlier.

But then, like a second sunset,
Inevitability descended,
Compelling me to gather my essence,

Abandon that tranquillity,
Walk the half-minute from the restaurant
To my cabin on the shore, seek sleep.

Tonight, lamenting my isolation from nature,
My loneliness, in this noisy St. Louis café,
I walk home, to last Friday's twilight.

The Village, the Lake, and the Woods

I. On First Returning

So where does one go first,
On arriving just after two, on a Wednesday afternoon,
If he has a mean hunger to feed?

Where else but the only place to grab lunch,
In a sleepy town this small:
The beer-and-whiskey-reeking Waterfront Bar & Grill,

Its facade leaning into East Waterfront Drive,
Its back deck stumbling down to the lake —
This tavern that moonlights, days, as an eatery,

And flourishes, late beyond the other side of night,
As the unofficial city hall/auditorium/casino,
The place to be, even when the sun doesn't set.

I have a cornucopia of fried foods to choose from;
Soup du jour suits my shrinking appetite.
Before long, my hunger isn't quite so mean. I leave.

Now, I'm ready to go out on the town.
But where is it? It's fifty yards away — my cabin,
Where I'll sojourn, for five days,

Commune with the lake's ancient spirits,
Find equanimity, amidst its glistening ripples,
Which lay in icy wait, just weeks ago.

Now, I know why I didn't come here in March.
Imagine if all I could have done
Was stay holed up or walk on water.

II. Lone Loon

Last evening,
Between 8:00 and 9:30
(How immaculately late it stays light, up here,
Near the southernmost tip of Lake Superior,
In this Wisconsin of my aging sensibility),

I watched myself, or an eerie simulacrum of me,
In the shape of a lone loon
(I've been told these exquisite creatures mate for life . . .
No doubt, this is the same widower I've seen,
From this very vantage at water's edge, myriad years),

Stitch Lake Nebagamon into a tapestry,
Stretched smoothly within vision,
Of the most intricate design,
As it bobbed, then dove beneath the water,
Searching for fish, frogs, leeches, and snails,

Surfaced again, five, ten, twenty, fifty yards away,
Floating and diving, rising and floating and diving,
As if with obsessive, predestined prescience,
Creating, from its haunting loneliness,
An image that might sustain us, for our time together.

III. Red-Winged Blackbirds

I rise, into this soundless, cloudless dawn,
And try to tag along with the sun,
Hoping to stay at its side, absorb its warmth.

But before even starting,
The journey to day's destination ends right here,
Where I spend the core of the morning

Meditating on red-winged blackbirds
Congregating in, flitting from, last year's cattails
Withered along the shore bordering this cabin,

From whose porch, I, shirtless,
Exhilarated by 7:30's forty-five-degree chill,
Listen to their inspired, high-pitched "kong-ka-ree"s

And hope to learn, from their fleet convocations,
A pattern worthy of my memorizing,
So that, with their notes, I might compose a song.

IV. Like a Duck to Water

What an unexpected pleasure, for me,
When I chanced to see a trinity of ducks paddling along,
Seemingly heedless, insouciant
(Doubtless, they were preoccupied, feeding),
Leaving tiny wakes, in their passage.

And as I watched them navigate ever westerly,
Meandering out of my focus,
Toward the still-hibernating boys' camp,
Where memory keeps the ten-year-old in me alive,
I couldn't help envisioning that shy, husky kid,

Who, on his first summer away from home,
In his loneliness, almost every chance he had,
Took to the clunky, hand-operated side-wheel boats,
Like a duck to water,
Paddling along, close by the shore.

V. Overflow

Whose woods these are, I think I know . . .
They're mine,
This pink-marbled late northern dusk,

When every tree, shrub, and vine
(Sending out twigs, shoots, creepers, claspers)
Is just beginning its mystical budding —

Spring's rhapsodic awakening,
Its rousing from under a smothering cover
Of brown needles, cones, desiccated leaves.

Everywhere I turn, I discern stirring.
Creeks, rivulets, gullies, rills, and brooks,
Which, in summer, run dry, are rioting,

Transporting the bloated earth's overflow
Of rains and snows
Accumulated during the past six months,

All water surging through this dense surround,
Headed for, merging with,
Steadily rising Lake Nebagamon.

And to think that less than three weeks ago,
This teeming region's reservoir
Hadn't yet molted its icy carapace

And would have been totally unaccommodating,
In receiving this precious excess,
Which, when summer calls, it'll gladly give up.

Now, as pink sublimes into purple, then slate night,
I listen, intimately,
Hear all sixty-seven acres of the camp

Whispering to me, in this purlieu's mother tongue,
Confirming, for this momentary eternity,
That these renascent woods are mine.

VI. The Passing Past

Deep in these empty early-May woods,
The only trees that seem to be living,
Except for evergreens,
Are the dead ones,
Whose decaying trunks lie aslant,
Atop the soggy land —
Fallen sentinels of generations past,
Proclaiming, in their crumbling muteness,
The truth of the ages:
Everything must give way.

VII. The Lake

The lake, not thirty feet from my cabin,
Is ineffably sedate, this 9 a.m.;
Save for a loon's plaint, silence reigns.

What is it about water, rather than grass,
As a backyard, stretching peacefully
To the farthest margins of wonderment?

With a lake, there's no mistaking whose it is;
It's yours for the taking.
It quenches your spirit's thirst,

Every time you breathe it into memory.
Its mere being is miracle enough.
Tasting it, with your eyes, is ecstasy.

But synesthesia doesn't come easily,
To the distracted, the detached.
It takes a naked soul to embrace a lake,

Make love to its palpability,
Discover savoring its nearness is all there is
And that *is* is the rapture of serenity.

VIII. There

When you look for it —
That which you'll never find —
It'll be there, waiting for you.

IX. One of the Boys

For three days, I've traipsed these woods,
Seeing creeks and gullies alive with runoff rush,
Leafless trees budding subtly, a sigh at a time,

Perceiving a climacteric is nigh,
That humans — campers and counselors —
Will appear, fill this stillness,

Unleash, for two months of summer tumult,
Youth's energies and hubris, before retreating,
As they have, the past eighty years,

From nature's embrace, into urban insularity,
Leaving these woods, as always,
To the patterns of untrammeled existence.

Suddenly, I, like the trees, sense an imminence.
It's me. I'm a benign interloper, too,
One of those boys, grown up, old, come home.

X. The Village

Perhaps as many as four hundred houses
Dotting this village and surrounding the namesake lake;
A constable, two deputies, a dozen volunteer firemen;
Four churches; a boys' summer camp; one bank;
A lone dentist; a post office; a public auditorium;
Two bars; a laundromat/carwash; a pastry shop;
A seasonal Dairy Queen and one full-service restaurant.
No schools or auto-repair garage; no doctors.
Thank God for the gas station/convenience-and-grocery store. . . .

Whatever this isolated community lacks
Is its greatest saving-grace asset:
That essentiality which always calls me back,
Asks me to place my trust in its safekeeping,
For days, a week (months on end, in my fantasies) —
This refuge that doesn't traffic in traffic,
Racket, pollutant-hazed skies,
Or the modern Protestant ethic of frenetic shopping.
Time itself vacations here, to catch its breath.

XI. The Lord of the Forest

From my disappearance, yesterday, into the woods,
I rematerialized with two souvenirs,
To prove, to disbelievers, that I'm a forest wizard

Who can camouflage himself, at will,
Blend in with, possess and be possessed by,
The essences of Norway spruces, red maples,

Assume the identity, ego, and personality
Of sunlight crashing, helter-skelter, through trees,
Transposing itself into the cacophony of mad shadows

Chasing their shadows in and out of the canopy,
Pretending to be lords of the forest, like me,
Governing the lives of mosses, fungi, and lichens.

Poised before me, on the kitchen table, are those amulets —
A cone I plucked from a balsam fir
And a scroll of bark I peeled from a white birch —

Totems conveying to me, in their native voice,
A language of love I know I'll always speak
Whenever I disappear into the woods.

XII. Bridge of Sighs

This morning (oh, how very long ago it seems),
I crossed the Bridge of Sighs
Connecting the village of Lake Nebagamon with Duluth

(Wisconsin with Minnesota, both with St. Louis),
That span separating me from the past six days,
When I reconnected with myself,

Sought the wise advice of an oracular lake,
Listened to its gentle, nurturing conversations
With hooded mergansers, great northern divers,

Spoke face to face — as if engaging God —
With graceful eighty-foot Norway spruces, balsam firs,
Two-centuries-old red and white pines,

Communed with my solitudinous, naked anima
(The wellspring of my lonely poetic soul),
Which claims suzerainty over my bones, my flesh,

Comprehending, for the first time in a long time,
That there's something fundamentally wondrous
About the vitalizing sensual and emotional joy

Humans, like other yearning creatures,
Should be entitled to seek out —
The absolutely primal rapture of happiness.

Now, back in my apartment, I weep —
A prisoner who, having crossed the Bridge of Sighs,
Left himself on the other side.

XIII. Path

Waking, raising the shade,
This first morning home,
Hoping to gaze, again, from my cabin,

All I can see, to my dismay,
Through the north-facing window,
Is a cityscape's high-rise gravestones —

A necropolis about to open for business —
And a sun climbing out of a Wisconsin lake,
Dazzling a path back to where my spirit flows.

The Cabin

I. The Beckoning

When lethargy, apathy,
And, in the final throes of dispassion, inertia
Bring your stifled spirit to its knees,

You know it's time to change routine's routine,
Light out for the territory beyond the city,
Make a clean break with reality's immediacy,

Let your psyche assume an identity you dreamed of being,
Once upon a comic-book or fairy-tale fantasy,
Or just go incognito, beneath singing trees and skies —

A shadow, a breeze, a whiff of pine,
A squint of sunlight skittering over a lake's silvery surface,
A sibilant secret from a full-blooming orange moon.

You always seem to sense when a lingering malaise
Finally beckons you to get away, escape,
Leave ennui behind, for an eon of hours, days.

And it's then that your blood seeks freedom's headwaters,
Flows upstream, bursting its banks,
Every mile of the journey back to your heart's tomorrow.

II. Floating Upstream

Having dinner by myself, in a local café,
Sipping wine, in hope of relaxing,
Decompressing from the rigors of my day labors,

I allow myself to dream of my imminent visit
To the tiny village of Lake Nebagamon,
In northern Wisconsin, a forty-minute drive east of Duluth,

And begin to feel my ligaments, tendons, muscles
Loosening, releasing their strangleholds
On my exhausted body's bones.

Tomorrow shall indeed be a red-letter day,
A jubilee dedicated to casting off apathy's shackles,
Seeking peace, rest, harmony with nature,

With the demons of my fired spirit, existence,
Obsessed with domesticating an untamable psyche —
The mind God deeded me, to create poetry,

From birth to death, dawn to dusk, eternally,
Abstract thought to concrete imagistic evocation,
Line by internally rhyming line, word by syllable, phoneme.

Gradually, I sense my soul coming into focus,
Inviting my fleshly essence to let go,
Accept the truth of this moment so nigh,

Float upstream, from St. Louis, past La Crosse, to Itasca,
And back down, to Lake Nebagamon,
Where, tomorrow, I'll reach shore . . . transcendence.

III. Second Try

Even though Lake Nebagamon isn't the Quetico,
Whose terraqueous wilderness
Is interconnected by a labyrinth of voyageurs' portages,

It can still be relatively difficult to reach,
Especially when you're trying to fly into Duluth,
Just west of this off-the-beaten-retreat,

And a thick fog, undergirded with rolling mists,
Enshrouds Lake Superior, making landing treacherous,
Sends your plane packing, back to Minneapolis,

To let you wait out the elements, at a safe distance,
And restrategize getting there,
Should nature decide not to cooperate

And reduce your grandiose escape plans
To spending the night in a nearby hotel
Or bedding down, with your frustrations, in the airport,

Instead of arriving (as you did, on the second try),
Then driving east, to Lake Nebagamon,
In time to enter the vast forest of northern stars.

IV. Tree Rings

Though I was just here one month ago,
Living out my entire life, in seven days, beside the lake,
Rummaging, each afternoon, through the woods
That cloak the boys' summer camp in privacy,
Everything, except my high-spirited excitement, has changed.

The village is filled, to bursting, with lilac trees
Spilling their pungent ivories, purples, and pale pinks,
In luxuriant excess, for the eyes to smell,
The nose to taste, the ears and tongue to touch, to see,
And the mind to revel in, with indulgent abandon.

The air is an ecstasy of songbird clarinets and flutes,
An entire woodwind symphony tuning up —
Robins, purple finches, evening grosbeaks,
Chickadees, juncos, white-throated sparrows —
And, everywhere, the leitmotif: "kill-dee-kill-dee-kill-deeee."

Just down the road, where East Waterfront Drive dead-ends
And Camp Nebagamon's rear gate swings open wide,
Docks are in the process of being put in, secured;
Canoes are out of storage, back in their racks;
Sailboats are bobbing, tugging at their buoys.

Throughout the cabin-scattered property, just stirring,
Counselors are preparing their project sites
Or (first-timers, anyway) introducing themselves
To the spruces and pines, the poplars, birches, and ashes,
Fending off swarms of merciless mosquitoes.

Unnoticed by most of them, unknown to all but a few,
I go about my meandering way,
Assessing the season's new whorls, sprigs, buds, cones,
Knowing that, within a week, the boys will arrive,
Adding another ring to their maturing trunks.

As for me, I realize, all too poignantly,
That I've attained my height, am shrinking, by degrees,
Drooping slightly, slowly decaying, from within,
And that my roots have begun to pull loose.
Perhaps that's why I come back here, year after year —

To commune with the child still alive inside me,
Who, at ten, was planted in this land,
Amidst majestic stands of red and white pine trees,
And who yet believes that enduring equanimity
Attends those who remain devoted to nature.

V. The Loons of Lake Nebagamon

Now, it's nine, nine-thirty, and, still, there's afterglow,
Diminishing, thinning out, yet lingering,
As though not wanting to go home —

Light left as testimony to a setting sun
Reluctant to abandon land that worships its warmth.
The sky's cathedral is inlaid with tesserae-clouds.

By ten, the looming gibbous moon,
Sensual and soft, in her naked tumescence,
Dominates the welkin — night's noble matriarch.

Stars more numerous than the shore's sand grains
Or the riffles on the water's stippled surface
Populate the rotunda, below whose vaulted ceiling I sit,

Gazing toward the heavens, from my seat on this dock,
Listening to the glistering silence,
Punctuated by the choiring of tree frogs,

And, intermittently, by the signifying and response
Of Lake Nebagamon's loons,
Who fill this wondrous evening, with their beautiful music,

Calling to each other, from coverts along these shores,
Unloosing their wails, yodels, tremolos, and hoots,
Composing a fugue not even Bach could have imagined.

And here I am, perhaps the only human on this whole lake
Who's outdoors, tonight, attuned to this magic,
Taking time to look and listen, see and hear.

VI. The Storm

This vigilant Friday night,
The wild, violent, white-frothing waves,
Driven by forty-mile-per-hour gusts, have finally died down.

The relative quietude those winds have left, in their wake,
Bequeaths the lake an incongruous calm,
Cautions those who populate its shores to be skeptical,

Question whether the worst is really behind us
Or if the daylong scourge,
Which gave even the loftiest pines, spruces, balsams pause,

Won't decide, later this evening, to redouble its vengeance,
Deliver this sodden region a knockout blow
Replete with wind devils and waterspouts.

How does one know, and what can be done?
Humans, and nature itself, are in fate's hands.
Despite all our advances, randomness rules the land.

VII. Right at Home

Just now, another day in Lake Nebagamon
Is preparing to welcome in another peaceful eventide,
Recite its prayers for a serene end of the week.

I, an outsider in this village so far north,
Feel, oddly, right at home, providential,
Not aloof, despite my privacy, my seeming pariahhood.

Indeed, in this enclave of about a thousand people,
I find my urban misanthropy dissipating,
My cynical psyche snuffing Diogenes's lantern,

No longer hoping to find one honest human being,
In the rat race's daylight I left behind,
Rather jettisoning my obsession with judging others.

After all, growing old brings with it some consolations,
Not the least of which is signing a truce with death,
Accepting snow in June and full moons at noon

And choosing the territory to which I might light out,
In search of happiness, joy,
The sanctity of silence born of a buoyant spirit.

VIII. By Myself

Waking up in my cabin,
Nibbling on a few cashews, for breakfast
(I have to be judicious — they're highly addictive),

Sipping from a mug of fresh-brewed decaf,
At the kitchen table, where I sit naked,
Bare feet warm on the cold linoleum floor,

Firing up my life-force's vital juices
(Senses, instincts, emotions, memory, intellect, imagination),
To engage in escape, through creative contemplation . . .

These are as close to glory as I can possibly get.
This quiet, priceless timelessness,
Which inspires me whenever I wake up by this lake,

Provides my spirit with everything it's been missing
Since long before I ever understood
That only in being by myself can my soul come to know me.

IX. Poet in a Cabin

The Spartan heart in me can endure starvation
For what might seem, to others, an eternity of hours,
Going without nourishment, through late afternoon,

The fasting stimulating my senses,
While leaving my flesh and bones to make do,
Live off their reserves of energy.

And why do I pursue this, purposely go hungry,
Inflict such deprivation on myself —
Exhilarating abstinence — when isolated in this cabin?

Why, indeed, if not to put my will on notice
That the only sustenance it needs
Must be harvested from the gardens deep in its keeping.

X. Camping in the Wilderness

This relaxed Sunday morning,
I'm attuned to the omnipresence of the prismatic lake,
Inviting me to come down to water's edge
And partake in a service of ecumenical worship,
A natural communion.

But I hesitate, so enchanted, yet, are my olfactories,
By the lingering aroma of olive oil and garlic,
Clinging to every inch of space in this cabin
(My idea of a tiny island campsite in the Quetico),
Where, last night, I prepared an "open fire" feast for myself.

Over the kitchen stove, I began my orchestration,
Bringing four quarts of water to a rolling boil
Before adding a package of whole-grain penne pasta,
Letting it boil again, then draining it off,
While I entered into more complex negotiations:

Dicing five cloves of garlic,
Sautéing them in a pan of extra-virgin olive oil,
Mixing in eight mushrooms sliced in quarters,
Then blending in steamed asparagus —
Each element carefully timed, according to my recipe.

And when I finished this ritual, merged the ingredients,
And slid the large pot onto the back burner's low heat,
I grabbed, from the icebox, the sirloin steak —
A thick, exquisitely marbled cut, perfect for grilling —
And headed out to the deck, then down to the pit,

Whose briquettes I'd set aglow, thirty minutes earlier,
With my version of flint and steel: lighter fluid and match.
Soon, those eight ounces were sizzling.
Above me, the moon hovered, in a mellow, fuzzy haze,
Casting a steppingstone path halfway across the lake.

I could have sworn it was inviting me to follow,
But I couldn't be distracted from my night's pleasures —
By then, it was ten o'clock; I had a hearty appetite.
(After all, a voyageur's life, out on the trail,
Is hardly an easy enterprise,

And invariably, by day's end, exhaustion sets in,
From the revitalizing fatigue of packing, paddling, portaging.)
Suddenly, along the shoreline, across from my cabin,
Possibly disturbed by a lone motorboat edging too close,
Invisible loons set loose a paroxysm of calls,

An evocative cacophony of echoes and volleys —
Hoots and wails and tremolos and yodels —
That resonated, in my mind, for at least an hour,
If not all night, in my sleep,
Even after their purgations of ecstasy or fear had faded.

I could tell, by the color of the steak,
That my moment of celebration was nigh.
The kitchen windows were fogged with pungent steam.
No scent ever smelled better to my craving taste buds.
With wine, I toasted my wilderness, and in peace, I ate.

XI. Sweet Time

Perhaps all of it, the searching for solitude,
Has everything to do with aging, edging graveward,
As though youth were an obstacle in its path,

An impediment to achieving some semblance of harmony,
An abiding sense of humanity,
Gaining a deep understanding of our place in the cosmos,

Taking solace in knowing we're significant,
At least insofar as we deem that our reason for being
Holds meaning for ourselves, if not for others.

In the early seasons, the first thirty or forty years,
Our frantic rush to assert independence, dominance,
Gain prominence, stockpile pleasures, material amenities,

Distracts us from our long-term objective.
We're blinded by our shortsighted visions of life,
And, yet, how could it be otherwise?

Peace is a quality we have to seek and find
Not in Scripture, poetry, hand-me-down philosophies,
But in ourselves, in our own sweet time —

A state of mind in which the eye can see sun shafts
Streaming down, through twilight clouds,
On soft breezes kissing a lake's ancient flesh,

Or catch fragments of an audaciously hued rainbow
Descending, from black rain clouds amassing in the west,
Directly into Lake Nebagamon's soul,

Or gaze at a halo of shimmering, iridescent ice crystals
Forming a primeval wheel around a full moon,
Capable of moving it through the universe, forever . . .

That inner eye, which sees the beginning of Creation,
Whenever we ask it to redeem us,
From mental and spiritual emptiness, through contentment.

XII. Surprise and Delight

Everything in nature —
That which resides outside my everyday cityscape —
Comes upon me, with mesmerizing surprise and delight,

As was the case with yesterday's late-afternoon rainbow
And with last midnight's lunar corona,
Looking up at itself, from the waves, like an iridescent eye,

And as is the case with this morning's sighting,
Just below my cabin, along the shoreline's sedgy stretch,
Of a commotion of waterfowl

Materializing, out of Lake Nebagamon's still surface,
Perhaps five or ten minutes earlier
Than my instincts, intuitions, could alert me

That I had unbidden visitors to quietude's preserve,
In which I'd sequestered my senses,
For the intense purpose of uprooting a poem, from the earth.

Stunned by the presence of so many Canada geese
(A trio of families boasting both parents,
Each with a brood of two, three, or four goslings),

I left off my labors, primed by pure excitement,
To spy on those beautiful creatures,
Who surely had no awareness of my presence —

Birds going about their business of being, feeding,
Keeping a very wary eye out, while foraging,
For predators lurking beyond those grassy stands.

And through the kitchen windows,
As intimately as my binoculars could make me privy,
I witnessed those nine downy babies

And those six magnificent adults,
With long black necks, white cheeks, elongated bills,
Brown-mottled wings, black tail-plumage,

Feast on the vegetation bordering the shore,
Slip into the water, the young ones diving, rolling over,
Climbing out, to pluck more lush seed sprouts,

Before finally moving on, floating out into the waters,
Farther and farther, even beyond my magnified range,
Until I was left alone, again, in quietude's preserve,

Alone but not quite the same,
For having felt surprise and delight come upon me,
As they do with rainbows, coronas, and other divinities.

XIII. At the Opera

I must admit I'm no avid bird watcher,
And yet, sitting here, this evening, at dock's end,
120 feet out, into the lake, at eight o'clock,

With reflections of shore-bordering red and white pines
Reaching far beyond me,
I listen to the birds — song sparrows, mainly —

Performing the most melodious arias conceivable,
More sonorous, lyrical, mellifluous
Than any Rossini, Verdi, or Scarlatti ever composed.

And at this immaculately gold-glowing dusky hour,
I revel in being an audience of one,
In my own outdoor La Scala,

Feeling moved not to *Pagliacci* sadness
But gentle orgasms of deep-throbbing joy —
Rapture capturing the passion of this moment's happiness.

XIV. Warmth

This robin's-egg-blue Tuesday morning,
The lake's surface is as smooth as the sky,
And the air is ashimmer with warmth.

After being here nearly a week,
I consider myself a villager in good standing,
A grateful ghost of the boys' camp down the road.

By this time tomorrow, I'll be gone from here,
On my way back home.
God knows, the prospect weighs heavy on my heart.

But for the remainder of this peerless day,
I'll invoke my most complex legerdemain,
To confuse demons who would confuse me,

Persuading me that I'm crazy,
For having ever even left civilization
Just for the sake of seeking a spot of repose,

A remedy, no matter how ephemeral,
That might save my soul from its urban blight,
Provide me a retreat in which to map time's trails.

Right now, I plan to explore glory's hinterlands,
Hold hands with, embrace, kiss, make love to the lake,
The woods, the village, this warm, cloudless sky.

XV. The Last Morning

I arise, this last morning
Of my most recent northern-Wisconsin incarnation,
To a lake as placid as liquid silence.

The kitchen windows, through which my vision lifts,
Are swarming with mosquitoes,
Which bite everything, in their desperation to thrive.

Now, I enact my favorite a.m. ritual:
Placing six spoonfuls of decaf into the coffee maker,
Filling it, waiting for it to hiss, grumble, groan,

Then pouring my first savory cup of the day
And toasting the sky, the lake, myself.
As I do so, a flotilla of Canada geese glides by —

The same three families, with their nine goslings,
I watched, just mornings ago,
Consume the seedy marsh grass just below my cabin.

I pass, on my breakfast of cashews, reconsider,
Then grab a handful and nibble like a squirrel.
This will be my last food, until tonight,

Since eating upsets my bodily rhythms, on flying days,
And moving through airports dispirits me,
Disorients my sense of being. I prefer staying put.

So why, then, I ask myself, am I leaving this land,
Where, last evening, I had a front-row seat
In which to watch the moon rise

From deep orange, through yellow, to ivory,
While I barbecued steak
And witnessed giddy staffers from the boys' camp

Walk up East Waterfront Drive, the quarter mile to the village,
For a last-minute spell of revelry
In the two bars or at the Dairy Queen,

Before the arrival of their charges, this afternoon
(At which time, I'll be back in St. Louis, doomed to routine) . . .
Why do I have to leave?

After all, for me, who's been excessively deskbound,
Just finding one retreat of this kind, in a lifetime,
Should be reason enough to strengthen my resolve

To change everything I've ever believed.
Gazing, dismayed, forlorn, out over the lake, beyond,
I pray being home will only be a temporary stay.

XVI. Coming Back

Year after year of desperate escape and relieved return,
I've always caught myself repeating a trite-but-true phrase:
"It's good to get away, but it's great to be home."

Only, tonight, on coming back from Wisconsin,
Where I sojourned in Lake Nebagamon's reaches,
Free to spend my time as I pleased, at my leisure,

I find everything turned inside up, outside down.
I'm bewildered, stunned, deflated,
Feeling that my immediate reality hardly satisfies me.

Indeed, I'm unenthralled, disenchanted, despondent.
My luxurious art-filled apartment repulses me.
On turning the key, for the first time in a week,

I was startled, appalled, by all my things.
Could it be that, while I was away,
Something defining, transformative, happened to me,

That a metamorphosis, mystical yet real, possessed me,
An epiphany, a reawakening, was born to me,
As I translated nature into my heart's genealogy?

Whatever's the case, knowing I'm no longer young,
Haven't been flexible, capable of change, for some time,
I'm yet inclined to read these negative emotions positively,

Extrapolate, from them, something wondrous to come,
In whatever's left of my future.
Were I to venture a tea-leaf reader's guess,

The best I might proffer would be this assessment:
I'd not feel surprised, not in the slightest,
If I held a spur-of-the-moment yard sale,

Pulled up tent stakes, packed a bag,
And headed back to the enclave of Lake Nebagamon,
To spend my remaining fecund days

Recording the diving and resurfacing, the tremolo, of loons,
The sacredness of crappies, bluegills, perch
Feeding at twilight, lip-rippling the water's surface,

The rainbow of full moons, the authority of Norway spruces,
The primordiality of mosquitoes, sumac, lichens, moss,
The morality of pine martens, chipmunks, skunks.

This Wednesday, my first night back, dining out,
I'd like, more than I can describe,
To be coming home to my cabin by the lake,

That place where something consequential, critical, crucial
Manifested itself to my unconscious,
Whispered, in my psyche's stone-deaf ear,

That, sooner than humanly possible,
I'd better get back to northern Wisconsin and stay there,
To share in the unfolding of my long-withered soul.

Autumn Comes
to Lake Nebagamon

I. Finding My Place

Were it not for the thirty-five-mile-per-hour gusts
Stirring up the air, to a majestic turbulence,
Tuning the trees to a melodic cacophony,

This incandescent Lake Nebagamon afternoon,
These sixty-six degrees
Would actually be, if it's possible, almost too hot.

As was the case on my last visit, this past June,
The lake's surface is a frenzy of argenteous water spirits.
Only, this time, they recognize me; I'm certain of it.

But for all its boisterous noise,
This hazy-blue, sun-blazing Thursday
Finds its place so easily, so palpably, so naturally,

In the sheltering realm of my being,
I might never have left here, three months ago.
Maybe, this trip, I won't go home.

II. Surprised

I don't know why I should be so surprised,
But I am, my cherished lake,
Surprised and extremely relieved, at the same time,

To see that you're still right here,
Precisely where I left you, in memory's keeping,
When I left you, last.

Ah, but that's just it, isn't it?
Lately, forgetting has been ravaging my domain,
Taking its toll on my cherished holdings,

Not least my hopes, my reveries, my dreams.
Even my capacious imagination
Has been ransacked by that mindless rapaciousness.

So maybe you can understand, even empathize,
When I express my surprise, my appreciation,
Especially over things I deeply treasure,

Like you, lake, my favorite place in my estate,
You matrix of my coming of age.
I pray you'll never evaporate.

III. Poet and Egret

Egret, egret, you great white egret,
You strange, gawky, ungainly giraffe of a bird,
Standing there, just up the shore from my dock,
On those glossy black stalks that seem anchored in concrete,
All of you motionless, save for that elongated neck
And yellow-billed head, with surveillant eyes,
Sweeping ceaselessly, like a lighthouse beacon.

Egret, egret, what kind of an existence is this,
That you pass your hours, in stasis, isolation,
Waiting for something to transpire, catch your attention,
Cause you to spurn inertia,
Set those stems in motion, release those wings,
Take flight, in search of life's vital inklings?
Could it be that, in you, I see a semblance of me?

IV. The Boys, the Leaves, and Me

My walk through the woods enveloping Camp Nebagamon
Is a blessing as well as a desolate undertaking.
I've been craving partaking of these rich environs,

All the while knowing that, in doing so,
I'd have to listen to the noise of invisible boys at play,
Lingering in this silent-singing place,

And contend not only with their haunting presence
But my own, from so many years ago,
When I spent fourteen summers here, discovering myself.

As I wander, the leaves, many still green,
In this beginning of the winnowing,
Myriad others assuming the dazzling dapplings of decay

(Sugar and red maples turning, in nature's kaleidoscope,
From viridescence, through orange, to blazing regal crimson;
Pin oaks taking on the same hues, less dramatically;

American basswoods yellowing mutedly, translucently;
Staghorn sumacs donning scarlet shrouds;
Balsams, spruces, pines witnesses to the vibrant dying) . . .

The leaves seem to be falling in line, behind me,
Following my circuitous maneuverings through camp,
As though I were a nurturing counselor,

Leading them on their first hike through this sacred garden,
Promising them that, come next spring,
We'll be back where we started on this late afternoon.

V. Another Day's Passing

From my table on this spacious wooden deck
Wrapping around the back of Lawn Beach Inn,
Facing a lake anticipating another sun's spectacular plunge
Into the pine-lined horizon bordering the shore,
Another ivory moon's rise, over those same trees,

I survey the majesty of this anonymous village,
This sparsely populated refuge from the world at large,
Where I've come to disappear from whoever I was
Before I decided, in late middle age,
To barter my earthly estate, for a sunset or three of repose,

And I realize that the unpredictable remainder of my life
Is already in play, fulfilling its complicated destiny,
Trying to conclude whether I should go or stay,
Trust that my intuition is oracular, visionary,
Not just a fantasy fated to fade away, with the passing day.

VI. Lake Magic

Though I've been at the cabin not quite three days,
The lake's abracadabran incantations
Have worked their magic, on my brain.

Already, I can take the waves' temperature,
Chart the fever of their heart,
As though I were measuring my own blood's heat,

Read between the lines of passing clouds,
Deciphering the primeval strata of the planet's existence,
Which contain dreams my being has deposited,

And translate the most minuscule sparkling of stars,
Recreating, from the celestial palimpsest,
A history of every moment in the annals of agelessness.

Yet what will remain for me to ascertain,
When I leave these shores, next week,
Is whether these newly gained powers will persist

Or dissipate to the point where I can't even see,
Let alone conjure, waves, clouds, stars,
For the black magic of the city's malevolent spells.

VII. Eloquence

Most people who own docks on Lake Nebagamon
Employ them for tying up boats
And as platforms from which to fish, at dusk,
The setting sun and rising moon
Mere backdrops for drinking beer and gabbing.

When I'm here, I gravitate toward dock's end,
Just to sit with open notebook, pen in hand,
And contemplate the grandeur of this tranquillity,
Hopeful that my spirit, longing for epiphany,
Might approximate nature's eloquence.

VIII. The Leaves

The peacefulness of this Sunday-morning village,
Now that the summer vacationers have departed
And autumn is creeping out of its leaves,
Cannot be fully appreciated in human measures;
The serenity of the changing landscape is just too ethereal.

Save for a lone bell, chiming its churchgoers to services,
The only sounds are those of the transfiguring leaves,
Whispering their deciduous threnodies,
Just weeks from fluttering down, to kiss the ground,
Receive reprieve from their timebound tethering.

And then there's me, who's never been a free spirit,
Located here not quite by sheer coincidence,
Whose wish has been to go with the drift of things —
A flesh-and-bones soliloquy,
Declaiming, to the leaves, to the breeze, my ecstasy.

IX. The Berry Pickers

My excursion from Lake Nebagamon, yesterday afternoon,
Was worth every second of the hour-and-a-half drive to Brule,
Then east, along Lake Superior's south shore,
Through the unincorporated communities
Of Port Wing, Herbster, and Cornucopia, to Bayfield,

Not so much for allowing me the opportunity
To contemplate the oceanic immensity of that freshwater body
But for letting me luxuriate in reminiscence,
Cast back to my first summer at the boys' camp,
When I, an introverted, self-conscious ten-year-old,

Spent half of one day, each week of the two-month session,
Picking blueberries, at Brule, with other less athletic kids,
Led by the camp's legendary director,
Max J. "Muggs" Lorber himself,
Who enticed us with promises of pies, that night, for dessert.

By the time I arrived at Blue Vista Farm,
Just outside the charming harbor-resort town of Bayfield,
Parked, surveyed the apple orchards overlooking the lake,
Admired the large, stone-and-wood-sided barn,
Where I got my requisite waxed box, I was primed,

Fully poised to indulge myself in a forgotten pastime,
Find, perhaps, in not-quite-idle preoccupation,
Something I might have left behind, in my haste to grow up.
And there they were: row upon row of blueberry bushes,
Waiting for me to contribute to the harvesting.

I set about fumbling among the branches of one.
The berries let loose, of their stems,
With only the slightest prodding from fingers
That had last performed this task fifty-seven years before.
After a few minutes, my back asked me to sit down,

Continue my gleaning from a position more suitable to my age.
Then it was that I saw that berry picker from 1951,
Walking, groping, with his pail, through the wilds of Brule,
Searching for the sporadic laden bushes
(Things weren't so orderly, so guaranteed, in those days).

For an undisturbed hour, doubtless more,
With the sun's bracing chill warming my skin,
I exulted in filling that box, with those ripe indigo fruits,
Stopping, occasionally, to place one on my tongue,
Taste the mildly tart sweetness of its succulent meat.

Next thing I knew, my bounty had been weighed, paid for,
And my Bayfield idyll was finished.
All that was left to do was drive back to my cabin,
With my blueberries and that shy little boy beside me,
Both of us happy again, liberated by such a simple joy.

X. Bois Brule

In search of nothing more than myself,
I traveled the five miles, as the goshawk flies,
To the Winneboujou canoe landing, on the Bois Brule,
Just to stop for a while, stand there, mesmerized,
And watch the quick, rippling river
Meander through crosshatched forest shadows
Wandering down to the banks, to wade, cool off.

For what could have been mere minutes, lifetimes,
Just listening to that water skittering past me,
I actually began to believe I'd discovered,
If not the fountain of eternal youth,
At least the secret to the subtleties of aging gracefully,
What sages, contemplating time's passage, know:
Composure is in the soul of the beholder.

XI. Late-Afternoon Daydreaming, on the Dock

In the lone patriarchal white pine
(At least 150 feet high, two hundred years old)
In the lot next to my cabin,

There are a half-dozen or so vociferous crows
Frenetically flapping, from limb to limb,
Keeping vigil over something only they can fathom.

My eyes, drawn to the top of that vertiginous tree,
By the sound of the birds' black caterwauling,
Keep going higher and deeper, into the opalescent sky,

As if being invited to catch a ride
On one of the cumulus clouds swiftly drifting past,
Heading in a direction I've never charted,

Which should be perfect, regardless,
For where I'd like to end up, come sunset
(Let's just say I revel in taking my chances).

When vision finally climbs down the giant pine,
No crows are raucously caw-cawing.
Now, the waves, chasing those clouds, beckon me.

XII. Up All Night

Last evening, just around dusk,
I entered the quiescence of the boys' camp,
From the hill surmounted by the hibernating Big House.

And as I roamed through those abandoned surrounds,
Past the shuttered Swamper Village cabins
(Inhabited, ten months a year, by phantoms),

Then down to the tennis courts, lower diamond, shrine,
Out the range road, beyond the Axeman Village,
Before veering into the woods between me and the lake,

I pondered how this eighty-year-old community,
Consisting of perhaps a hundred structures,
Is a mirror image, albeit in microcosmic proportions,

Of the village of Lake Nebagamon itself —
An alter ego, a little brother,
The Big House its auditorium, the cabins its residences.

Just then, the breathing forest delivered me to the shore,
With barely five minutes to witness the flaming sun
Descend into the canopy of trees, on the near horizon,

Without setting the entire countryside on fire,
And leave, on the air, pink, purple, and orange smudges,
Its companionate swath flickering on the lake —

A shimmering bridge spanning the distance,
Not suggesting I cross it or turn my back
(That would have to be my decision, from start to finish).

Gradually, with a lover's subtle touch,
Nightfall laid its opaque cloak over the waiting land.
Soon they would be sleeping side by side, under the stars,

While I, my bone marrow, my blood, my very being,
Would still be energized by those muted hues,
Still be too ravished, by their beauty, to close my eyes.

XIII. Having Our Ways

From late last night,
Right on through this dull-gray Tuesday noon,
The wind has been pushing its raucous way around,

While I've hidden in this groaning, creaking cabin,
Satisfied to let it take the brunt of the lake's frontal assault,
And ridden out this persistent rain, without complaint.

With nowhere specific to go, no place I have to be,
No mandates to comply with, no reservations to arrive for,
What difference could my sublime submission possibly make?

Days like this have been strangers to my frenetic life,
Far too few to have even eluded memory.
In truth, their existence, over my sixty-seven years, is a fluke.

So if, after all this wasted haste I've left in my wake,
I choose to call a halt to the hours,
Stay holed up, gazing at the roiling lake, the blustery sky,

I'm damn well going to do as I damn well please,
Proclaiming, *This is* my *time,* my *freedom,* my *entitlement,*
To achieve enlightenment, just by letting the day have its way!

XIV. Autumnal Moods

This Wednesday a.m., at my water's-edge cabin,
The sky is so matchlessly golden
And the lake so serenely one with its shoreline,

You might never guess the tempest that possessed it,
All yesterday and throughout the loud night —
Those intractable, crashing squalls of pure fury,

The swashbuckling rain, which started at five,
Just as I began my hike through the boys' camp,
And soaked my shoes, clothes, my flesh, to its bones,

That storm, which, by a sodden eight o'clock,
When I hoped to barbecue fresh coho salmon,
Had transformed into a Wagnerian opera

Of martial thunder and demonic lightning bolts
Arcing across the dark heavens, like an apocalyptic army,
Threatening my cabin, with instantaneous incineration.

You might never guess that this silent, cloudless, blue sky,
This placid, sun-faceted lake,
These oaks, maples, sumacs, and basswoods

Flaunting their coat-of-many-colors robes,
As though celebrating the beguilingly dying leaves
Still within their northern territorial keeping,

Endured such violent riot, just yesterday,
Or that this calm, balmy, sunny Lake Nebagamon day
Will, too soon, be lashed, ravaged, by winter's wrath.

XV. Sundowns

Tonight, just into my 7:20 flight out of Minneapolis,
Returning from the north country's glories,
I'm already sensing a melancholy emptiness
Welling in the pit of my spirit,
Threatening to make me soul-sick for Wisconsin.

Off to my right, a striated layer of colossal light,
Ranging hundreds of miles along the western horizon,
Hypnotizes the sky, with its voluptuous hues —
Reds, pinks, roses, oranges, peaches, purples, indigos, violets —
Lending, to twilight's denouement, a spectacular coda.

Tracking it halfway back to St. Louis,
I no longer feel so disconsolate, somber, lonely,
As though that elongated glow, seen at 31,000 feet,
Were following me, guiding me home,
While tying my heart to Lake Nebagamon,

Where, for five of the last six evenings,
I watched the sun descend into forests bordering the water,
On whose shores I stood ravished, breathless,
More certain than ever before
That, finally, I'd found the locus of my life's quest.

Poem Suites

The chapters in this volume reflect the structure of poetry suites Louis Daniel Brodsky wrote during visits to Lake Nebagamon, Wisconsin. The dates of composition for these suites are as follows:

Late September (9/21–24/06)

Lake Nebagamon Sojourn (7/14–23/07)

The Woods (9/6–14/07)

The Village, the Lake, and the Woods (5/7–13/08)

The Cabin (6/11–18/08)

Autumn Comes to Lake Nebagamon (9/18–24/08)

Biographical Note

Louis Daniel Brodsky was born in St. Louis, Missouri, in 1941, where he attended St. Louis Country Day School. After earning a B.A., magna cum laude, at Yale University in 1963, he received an M.A. in English from Washington University in 1967 and an M.A. in Creative Writing from San Francisco State University the following year.

From 1968 to 1987, while continuing to write poetry, he assisted in managing a 350-person men's-clothing factory in Farmington, Missouri, and started one of the Midwest's first factory-outlet apparel chains. From 1980 to 1991, he taught English and creative writing, part-time, at Mineral Area College, in nearby Flat River. Since 1987, he has lived in St. Louis and devoted himself to composing poems and short fictions. He has a daughter and a son.

Brodsky is the author of sixty-four volumes of poetry (five of which have been published in French by Éditions Gallimard) and twenty-four volumes of prose, including nine books of scholarship on William Faulkner and eight books of short fictions. His poems and essays have appeared in *Harper's*, *Faulkner Journal*, *Southern Review*, *Texas Quarterly*, *National Forum*, *American Scholar*, *Studies in Bibliography*, *Kansas Quarterly*, *Forum*, *Cimarron Review*, and *Literary Review*, as well as in *Ariel*, *Acumen*, *Orbis*, *New Welsh Review*, *Dalhousie Review*, and other journals. His work has also been printed in five editions of the *Anthology of Magazine Verse and Yearbook of American Poetry*.

In 2004, Brodsky's *You Can't Go Back, Exactly* won the award for best book of poetry, presented by the Center for Great Lakes Culture, at Michigan State University.

Other Poetry and Short Fictions Available from Time Being Books

Yakov Azriel
Beads for the Messiah's Bride: Poems on Leviticus
In the Shadow of a Burning Bush: Poems on Exodus
Threads from a Coat of Many Colors: Poems on Genesis

Edward Boccia
No Matter How Good the Light Is: Poems by a Painter

Louis Daniel Brodsky
By Leaps and Bounds: Volume Two of *The Seasons of Youth*
The Capital Café: Poems of Redneck, U.S.A.
Catchin' the Drift o' the Draft *(short fictions)*
Combing Florida's Shores: Poems of Two Lifetimes
The Complete Poems of Louis Daniel Brodsky: Volumes One–Four
Dine-Rite: Breakfast Poems
Disappearing in Mississippi Latitudes: Volume Two of *A Mississippi Trilogy*
The Eleventh Lost Tribe: Poems of the Holocaust
Falling from Heaven: Holocaust Poems of a Jew and a Gentile *(Brodsky and Heyen)*
Forever, for Now: Poems for a Later Love
Four and Twenty Blackbirds Soaring
Gestapo Crows: Holocaust Poems
A Gleam in the Eye: Volume One of *The Seasons of Youth*
Leaky Tubs *(short fictions)*
Mississippi Vistas: Volume One of *A Mississippi Trilogy*
Mistress Mississippi: Volume Three of *A Mississippi Trilogy*
Nuts to You! *(short fictions)*
Once upon a Small-Town Time: Poems of America's Heartland
Paper-Whites for Lady Jane: Poems of a Midlife Love Affair
Peddler on the Road: Days in the Life of Willy Sypher
Pigskinizations *(short fictions)*
Rated Xmas *(short fictions)*
Rabbi Auschwitz: Poems of the Shoah
Shadow War: A Poetic Chronicle of September 11 and Beyond, Volumes One–Five
Showdown with a Cactus: Poems Chronicling the Prickly Struggle
    Between the Forces of Dubya-ness and Enlightenment, 2003–2006
Still Wandering in the Wilderness: Poems of the Jewish Diaspora
This Here's a Merica *(short fictions)*
The Thorough Earth
Three Early Books of Poems by Louis Daniel Brodsky, 1967–1969: *The Easy
    Philosopher*, *"A Hard Coming of It" and Other Poems*, and *The Foul Rag-
    and-Bone Shop*

Louis Daniel Brodsky (continued)

Toward the Torah, Soaring: Poems of the Renascence of Faith
A Transcendental Almanac: Poems of Nature
Voice Within the Void: Poems of *Homo supinus*
With One Foot in the Butterfly Farm *(short fictions)*
The World Waiting to Be: Poems About the Creative Process
Yellow Bricks *(short fictions)*
You Can't Go Back, Exactly

Harry James Cargas (editor)

Telling the Tale: A Tribute to Elie Wiesel on the Occasion of His 65th
    Birthday — Essays, Reflections, and Poems

Judith Chalmer

Out of History's Junk Jar: Poems of a Mixed Inheritance

Gerald Early

How the War in the Streets Is Won: Poems on the Quest of Love and Faith

Gary Fincke

Blood Ties: Working-Class Poems

Charles Adès Fishman

Blood to Remember: American Poets on the Holocaust *(editor)*
Chopin's Piano

CB Follett

Hold and Release

Albert Goldbarth

A Lineage of Ragpickers, Songpluckers, Elegiasts & Jewelers: Selected
    Poems of Jewish Family Life, 1973–1995

Robert Hamblin

From the Ground Up: Poems of One Southerner's Passage to Adulthood
Keeping Score: Sports Poems for Every Season

William Heyen

Erika: Poems of the Holocaust
Falling from Heaven: Holocaust Poems of a Jew and a Gentile *(Brodsky and Heyen)*

866-840-4334
http://www.timebeing.com

William Heyen (continued)
The Host: Selected Poems, 1965–1990
Pterodactyl Rose: Poems of Ecology
Ribbons: The Gulf War — A Poem

Ted Hirschfield
German Requiem: Poems of the War and the Atonement of a Third Reich Child

Virginia V. James Hlavsa
Waking October Leaves: Reanimations by a Small-Town Girl

Rodger Kamenetz
The Missing Jew: New and Selected Poems
Stuck: Poems Midlife

Norbert Krapf
Blue-Eyed Grass: Poems of Germany
Looking for God's Country
Somewhere in Southern Indiana: Poems of Midwestern Origins

Adrian C. Louis
Blood Thirsty Savages

Leo Luke Marcello
Nothing Grows in One Place Forever: Poems of a Sicilian American

Gardner McFall
The Pilot's Daughter
Russian Tortoise

Joseph Meredith
Hunter's Moon: Poems from Boyhood to Manhood
Inclinations of the Heart

Ben Milder
The Good Book Also Says . . . : Numerous Humorous Poems Inspired by
the New Testament

866-840-4334
http://www.timebeing.com

Ben Milder (continued)
The Good Book Says . . . : Light Verse to Illuminate the Old Testament
Love Is Funny, Love Is Sad
What's So Funny About the Golden Years
The Zoo You Never Gnu: A Mad Menagerie of Bizarre Beasts and Birds

Charles Muñoz
Fragments of a Myth: Modern Poems on Ancient Themes

Micheal O'Siadhail
The Gossamer Wall: Poems in Witness to the Holocaust

Joseph Stanton
A Field Guide to the Wildlife of Suburban O'ahu
Imaginary Museum: Poems on Art

Susan Terris
Contrariwise